# SLAY
## Your Day

PRESS START

GAME OVER

# OLIVIA MURRAY

# Welcome Readers!

In today's fast-paced world, it can be challenging to keep up with the demands of daily life. However, with the right strategies and mindset, you can take control of your time and achieve your goals. That's where this book comes in.

This comprehensive guide covers key themes and provides practical tips and techniques for you to implement in your own life, allowing you to make the most of each day and achieve more in less time.

By following the advice included, you too can enjoy the numerous benefits. Whether you are a student, a professional, a stay-at-home parent, or anyone in between, this book has something for all of you.

I know from experience that changing habits and routines can be challenging. That's why I designed this book to be an easy-to-follow guide with practical, actionable steps that you can take to improve your daily productivity and well-being.

I am excited to share this journey with you and to help you reach your full potential.

So, let's get started and **SLAY YOUR DAY!**

# I. Introduction

## A. The Purpose of The Book

The purpose of this book "Slay Your Day" is to help you improve your daily productivity and live your best life by teaching key organisation skills, the benefits of getting up early, the importance of focus, and the power of time blocking.

I am going to give you practical tips, techniques, and examples to implement these concepts in your own life and make the most of each and every day.

The ultimate goal here is to empower you to take control of your time and achieve greater success and satisfaction in your personal and professional life.

The key themes in the book we will discuss are:

*Organisation:* This theme focuses on the importance of being organised and provides guidance for getting to grips with your life by looking at creating to-do lists and decluttering. This will really help to reduce your stress that's for sure!

*Early Rising:* Here we discuss the concept of waking up early, with some handy, yet practical tips for becoming an early riser, including the science behind early rising and its benefits. I promise, it will be worth it.

*Focus:* The theme of focus explores the importance of avoiding distractions and maintaining focus in order to be productive and achieve your goals. This may seem straight forward, but there are some pitfalls to avoid.

*Time Blocking:* Probably my favourite chapter is on the power of time blocking and how it can help you make the most of each day. We will talk about creating an effective schedule, and I will tell you how this amazing method has helped me, and many other people slay their entire week!

These chapters come together to provide a guide for anyone looking to have their best possible day, which in turn will develop into your best weeks and months to come.

Overall, I want you to 'Slay' your entire LIFE! But for now let's take it one day at a time shall we?

# II. The Importance of Getting Up Early

## A. The Science Behind Early Rising

 I know that this is probably the last thing you want to hear, and you have probably heard it a million times before, but here are so many benefits to getting up early. This book is grounded in the science of productivity, and research has shown that people who wake up early tend to be more productive and more successful. One reason for this is that waking up early allows you to take advantage of your natural circadian rhythms, which are biological processes that regulate the body's internal clock.

The circadian rhythm is a 24-hour cycle that regulates various bodily functions, including sleep and wakefulness. Studies have concluded that waking up early can help you synchronise your circadian rhythm with the natural light-dark cycle, resulting in better sleep quality and improved stamina during the day.

In addition to the benefits of circadian rhythm synchronisation, waking up early can also provide you with more physical time to accomplish your goals. With more time at your disposal, you can engage in productive activities and prioritise your most important tasks before the hubbub of the day begins. This, in turn, leads to a greater sense of accomplishment and a great start to the rest of your day!

Furthermore, waking up early can also improve mental clarity and focus. The early morning hours tend to be quieter and less distracting than other times of the day, allowing you to focus on your tasks and work without interruptions such as the dog, the kids, or your partner!

Overall, the science behind early rising and productivity provides a compelling argument for why waking up early can be beneficial for you if are looking to achieve more. And the good news is, it doesn't have to be every day! Set yourself the mini goal of just one day a week to start, and by the time you see the benefits for yourself, you will be wanting to add more days in no time!

## B. The Benefits of Waking Up Early

So now we know that waking up early has some real science behind, it is including increased energy and reduced stress. By waking up early and exposing yourself to natural light, you can give your body a real boost of energy and start the day feeling refreshed and alert.

In addition to increased energy, waking up early can also help reduce stress. By giving yourself a head start to the day, you can avoid the rush of the morning and have more time to yourself for a coffee and a look over your to do list. (I call this my MAMA TIME!) Getting mentally prepped for the day ahead can help you feel more in control of your things and reduce the stress that often comes with feeling rushed and behind, and nobody's likes that do they?

Moreover, waking up early provides you with the opportunity to establish a routine and stick to it. Having a routine is essential in finding yourself able to be more productive and structure in your life is paramount to building a life you love.

## C. Practical Tips for Becoming an Early Riser

Becoming an early riser takes time, effort, and discipline, but with the right techniques, anyone can make it a part of their daily routine, even me! Here are some practical tips to help you get started:

1. Gradually adjusting your bedtime by 15-30 minutes each night can help you get used to waking up earlier. Aim to be in bed by 10-11 pm, so you can get the recommended 7-9 hours of sleep each night. (I have been known to go to bed by 9.00pm on some nights and the extra sleep has done me wonders!)

2. A dark, quiet, and cool environment can help you sleep better and wake up feeling refreshed. Make sure your room is dark, use earplugs or a white noise machine to block out noise, and keep the room at a comfortable temperature.

3. Establishing a bedtime routine for yourself can help signal to your body that it's time to sleep. This can include activities such as reading, stretching, or meditating. (I have a cup of bedtime tea and only drink at bedtime in my very special mug!)

4. The blue light emitted by screens can interfere with the production of melatonin, making it harder to fall asleep. Avoid screens for at least an hour

before bedtime. If you are like me and if affects you during the day too, consider getting a pair of blue light glasses to help.

5. Set an alarm clock to wake up at the same time each day, even on weekends. Gradually move the alarm clock earlier until you reach your desired wake-up time. It really helps to have a song or a sound to look forward to as well, I like to use Disney songs!

6. As we discussed earlier, exposure to natural light helps regulate your circadian rhythm and makes it easier to wake up. Try to spend time outside in the morning or open the curtains to let in natural light. I always open my curtains as soon as I get up, it's a good habit to get into.

By following these practical tips, you can gradually become and early riser and reap the benefits of waking up early. Why not just try them one at a time and once you have smashed one of them, add another until they are all part of your day.

Remember, it takes time and effort, but with persistence and discipline, you can do it!

# III. Organising Your Life for Maximum Productivity

## A. Benefits of Organisation

Face facts, when you are organised, you can prioritise tasks, keep track of important deadlines, and manage your time effectively. It is the key to slaying anything, not just your day! The idea is to no longer be overwhelmed by the sheer volume of tasks you need to complete but to structure them, and that is the way to organise.

Organisation also increases efficiency. You are less likely to waste time searching for lost items or trying to remember what you need to do next if the answer is laid out in front of you. A simple note in your planner can work wonders as a reminder of where you put things, and I always do this is if have filed away something I need later in a safe place (because I never remember my safe pace!)

In addition to the practical benefits, being organised can also boost confidence and self-esteem. Being able to positively effect your mental health is always worth taking the time to do, and when you feel a sense of accomplishment and pride in the work you have achieved your health is going to get better because of that.

## B. Simple Organisation Techniques

   This part can seem overwhelming, but I don't wasn't you to worry as there are simple steps you can use to get started, and we can take them one at a time.

*Planning*

Where would I be without my planner? Well, not writing this book that's for sure!

When I discovered planning for the first time I was a full time working Mama with two kids, a Husband and a dog. Living in a filthy house, eating takeaways and tripping over mountains of laundry. IT WAS CHAOS!

One day I had visited my local stationary store where I came across a beautiful planner, it was pink and silver (glittery of course) and I brought it without a second thought. It sat on my kitchen counter for nearly three weeks before I accidentally came across it again (I was looking for a letter I needed from school that I had lost) I had somewhat of an epiphany as I flipped through the pages of the planner. I noticed it came with one of those little wallets on the front, just perfect for storing those important papers and letters if I needed to find them. Why had I not done this before??

That very evening, I hunted around the house to find coloured pencils, crayons and highlighters and began to fill in my planner. I put on an episode of my show on Netflix and before I knew it I was there … organised for the first time in my life.

My planner was full of all the school dates, doctors' appointments, and holidays I had unloaded from my mind, and I felt relief, like a weight had been lifted off my shoulders. Could this little glittery book have now become an extension of my brain that I could add to when my actual brain was overloaded? The next few weeks saw me become the woman I am now. I took to planning like a duck to water and now, if it's not in my planner, its not in my life!

What I am trying to say, is if I had just used that darn planner the day I brought it, I would not have spent three days looking for a letter I had already sent back to school, and accused the kids, the dog and my poor Husband of all moving!

Planning really help even the most disorganised of people (like me) get to grips with this crazy thing called life. Give it a try!

*Creating A To Do List*

If mapping out your entire life in a planner is not for you then creating to-do list is a simple and effective way to get started. A to-do list allows you to keep track of all the tasks you need to complete, prioritise them, and make sure you don't forget anything important. You can create a to-do list each day, or at the beginning of the week, and update it as needed the choice is yours. I use a list on a daily basis and at the end of every day I roll over any tasks I have yet to do to tomorrow. I try and get at least my top three things done each day, but there are times I cross off nothing at all. Don't be too hard on yourself, we all have days when life gets in the way. Draw a literal line through it and try again tomorrow.

## Decluttering

I know this may be controversial but I do still like a bit of clutter in my house, it makes it feel like home. That being said, decluttering is another tool to get yourself and your life organised.

The process involves getting rid of items you no longer need or use, which can help free up space and reduce stress. Why not start by decluttering one room at a time or even one draw or cupboard first and focus on items you no longer need or use. This can include clothes, books, toys, and other items that are taking up space in your home.

There are several decluttering experts out there, but my favourite must be Marie Kondo. Marie, also known as KonMari, is a Japanese organising consultant, author, and television personality. She is best known for her method of organising, which she developed and popularised in her book "The Life-Changing Magic of Tidying Up: The Japanese Art of Decluttering and Organizing," published in 2014.

The KonMari method is a system of decluttering and organising that emphasises keeping only items that "spark joy" and discarding everything else. The method involves organising possessions by category rather than location and encourages people to thank items they are discarding for their service before letting them go.

I use Marie's methods often when I have a clear out. I literally empty the entire drawer or cupboard and ask myself with each item, 'Does it bring me joy?' If the answer is no, I look to donate it or recycle it if possible. If it's a yes, then I look to find it a more purposeful home.

So, I do still have some clutter, I just have clutter that brings me joy!

In addition to these options, there are many other simple ways you can use to get started along the way. For example, use folders or binders to organise important papers, and label items to make them easier to find. I like to use a filing case to keep things like our insurance documents, and medical information, stuff like that. I also keep an electronic copy filed in a similar way in a password protected folder on my computer, should I ever need a digital version.

One of the best resources for getting started with organising is Pinterest. It also happens to be one of my favourite sites in general.

Pinterest has some amazing ideas and inspiration for getting started with being an organisation guru, so why not take a look and you may come across something you love!

I want you to remember, the key is to start small and gradually incorporate these techniques into your daily routine.

## C. How to Prioritise

Prioritising tasks effectively is essential for making the most of your day and achieving your overall goals. Before I start on anything, I always assess what I have on and what is a must-do for the day. Whether it be an appointment, an important phone call or another deadline task, ensuring that these mini goals are met helps me balance my tasks and get things done in the right order. After all, it is easier to slip in a non-time related task, such as putting in a load of laundry or sweeping the floor around these time sensitive ones. Here are steps you can use to prioritise tasks effectively:

- Start by creating a comprehensive list of all the tasks that need to be completed. This includes everything from important work assignments to personal tasks. I like to separate my work tasks from my home ones, but the choice is up to you depending on how you want to work.
- Once you have your list, evaluate each task based on its urgency and importance. Urgent tasks are those that require immediate attention, while important tasks are those that will have a significant impact on your goals or objectives.

- Based on the urgency and importance of each task, assign a priority level to it. You can use a system like High, Medium, and Low or assign numbers 1-3 to each task to help you remember the order. Why not challenge yourself to complete your top three High level tasks, one of your Medium and two of your Low in one day? Make it a competition with yourself, but feel free to amend the number of tasks if you need to, it is important to not overdo it!
- Once you have prioritised your tasks, start working on the ones that are most important and urgent. These are the tasks that require your immediate attention and will have the most significant impact on your goals. Crossing these off as you complete them will also boost your morale and give you an incentive to get even more done.
- As a busy Mama I am testament to the fact that priorities can change quickly. It's important to reassess your priorities throughout the day. This will help you stay on top of your workload and ensure that you are always focusing on the most those high priorities.

I want you to remember that prioritising is a skill that takes practice, so be patient with yourself as you work to improve.

# IV. Staying Focused and Avoiding Distractions

## A. The Importance of Focus

Let's face it, life is busy and now more than ever it is so easy to lose focus. Without focus, you can easily become distracted, waste time, and fail to complete your mission of slaying your day!

Here are a few reasons why focus is important for productivity:

- Focus allows you to concentrate on one task at a time, which leads to increased efficiency and faster completion of tasks. When you are focused, you can give your full attention to a task, which helps you to get it done more quickly and effectively.
- Focus also allows you to give your full attention one thing at a time, which can lead to improved quality. When you are focused, you can pay closer attention to detail, which can help you produce a higher quality result.
- Lack of focus can lead to stress, as you struggle and begin to feel overwhelmed. Working with focus on the other hand, can reduce the level stress by you stay organised, on track, and in control.

- Believe it or not, focus can also boost creativity, as it allows you to experiment and come up with new ideas and solutions.

I know what you may be thinking at this stage, how can I possibly focus when the dog, the kids and your partner are all demanding your attention? The answer is practice. This step in the book probably took me the longest to master but I simply had to be strict with myself and with others. When you have an important task, not matter what it may be, only you can choose to focus on it. I found that being open and honest with my family and giving them a heads up if I had something that was time sensitive helped a lot.

I also try to give myself a little treat once I have completed my task (my go to was a fresh cup of coffee and a biscuit) as this made me have something to look forward to once the jobs were done.

## B. How to Overcome Distractions

Distractions are a common challenge that can impede your productivity and prevent you from making any headway. Here are some of the most common distractions and strategies for overcoming them:

- Technology, such as social media, emails, and the internet, can be a major source of distraction. They are the biggest competition I have in my household. To overcome these distractions, consider turning off notifications on your devices, using apps that block distractions, or dedicating specific blocks of time for checking emails and social media. I have been known just to take tech-free time altogether when everything goes off. Admittedly this was weird at first, but it has become time that I actually enjoy!
- Noise can be a major source of distraction, especially in open-plan offices. To overcome noise distractions, consider using noise-cancelling headphones or working in a quiet environment. In our house finding a quiet environment can be troublesome to say the least. As an example, why not consider moving to a different location if time will allow. Visit a local coffee shop, library or public space to complete tasks such as

working on emails from your computer or phone.

- Interruptions from co-workers or family members can be the biggest source of distraction. To deal with these interruptions, consider setting boundaries and communicating your needs clearly. You can also use door signs or headphones to signal that you are busy and cannot be disturbed. I saw an amazing hack on Pinterest which I often use at home. My home workspace is set up in a corner of our living room. So, I created a two-sided sign which I hang above my computer. One side says, 'Mama is busy come back later', and the other says, 'Mama is available for hugs'. By using this simple sign, my children have come to recognise the wording and colours that signal if they can interrupt me or not. Admittedly it took them a few tries to get the hang of it, but now it's common knowledge that if Mama is Out of Order, that I am in the zone and disturbing me would be unwise!

- Mental distractions, such as worries, thoughts, or emotions, can be a major source of distraction. To overcome mental distractions, consider practicing mindfulness, meditation, or other stress-management techniques. One of the ways I do this is with a pack of post it notes. Whilst I am working, if something pops up, I simply jot it down on a post it, allowing myself to acknowledge it but off loading it from my mind. I then give myself permission to deal with it later. I add it straight into my planner, shut it and forget about it. Then, when I refer to my planner later in the day I am reminded by the post it and can work the task into my plans for the day accordingly.

Distractions are a common challenge that can impede productivity. To overcome them consider using the strategies we have discussed here, or get online and do some research and see if there are any other ideas that you would like to try.

# C. Techniques to Improve Focus

Improving focus can be key to boosting productivity and achieving your desired outcomes. Here are a few more techniques you can try:

1. Mindfulness is the practice of paying attention to the present moment without judgment. This technique can help individuals improve focus by reducing distractions and increasing awareness of the present. To practice mindfulness, consider meditation, deep breathing exercises, or other mindfulness techniques. My Fitbit has a great little app that allows me to set some time for deep breathing. When I am feeling overwhelmed, I simply set it for a couple of minutes, and it helps ground me and change my strategy to get re-focused.

2. Perhaps try using positive affirmations. Positive affirmations are statements that can help you shift your mindset and stay focused on your goals. Repeating positive affirmations to yourself can help you stay motivated and focused on what you want to achieve. Repeating phrases like, *'I am focused, and I will complete this successfully'* can help boost morale and allow you to channel your energy into your current task.

3. Getting enough sleep has been a game changer for me. I was guilty or trying to survive on just 4-5

hours a night but it didn't realise the damage I was going to myself both mentally and physically. We spoke earlier in the book about the benefits of being an early riser, but to implement this you need to get enough sleep to begin with.

4. Exercise can help individuals improve focus by reducing stress, increasing energy, and improving overall well-being. To improve focus through exercise, consider a daily physical activity, such as running, yoga, or weightlifting.

At this stage I want to encourage you to experiment with different techniques until you find what works best for you. With consistent effort, you can improve your focus and achieve your goals.

# V. The Power of Time Blocking

## A. Explaining Time Blocking

Time blocking is a time management technique that involves breaking down your day into blocks of time and dedicating each block to a specific task or activity. I first came across this technique when I discovered one of my now favourite Youtuber's Jordan Page. Jordan Page is an American blogger, author, and public speaker who is known for her work in personal finance, budgeting, and family organization. She is the founder of the website and blog, "Fun Cheap or Free," where she shares her tips and strategies for living a frugal but enjoyable lifestyle.

Working with a blocking method helps you aids in prioritising tasks and focusing on completing them to the best of your ability with the time you physically have available. It's a great way to ensure you are not constantly switching between different things.

The idea is to set aside specific times for different activities and tasks, rather than simply working on things as they come up throughout the day. Here's an example of how time blocking works:

Let's say you have a busy day that includes several work tasks, household chores, and personal errands. To manage your time effectively, you could use time blocking to create a schedule that looks something like this:

6:00-7:00am: Exercise and get ready for the day

7:00-8:00am: Breakfast and family time

8:00-9:00am: Respond to important emails

9:00-11:00am: Work on a big project

11:00-12:00pm: Break and run errands

12:00-1:00pm: Lunch and family time

1:00-3:00pm: Work on another project

3:00-4:00pm: Household chores

4:00-5:00pm: Personal time

5:00-6:00pm: Dinner and family time

6:00-7:00pm: Planning for the next day

7:00-9:00pm: Personal time or family activities

9:00-10:00pm: Wind down and prepare for sleep

In this example, you have divided your day into specific time blocks for various activities, including work, household tasks, personal errands, and family time. By sticking to this schedule, you can ensure that you have enough time for each activity, and you can minimise distractions and interruptions by focusing on one task at a time.

I want to stress here that getting started in time blocking can be challenging but I can vouch for the huge benefits it can bring to your work and home life. The goal here is to create a more structured and intentional approach to your daily routine. If you can implement it successfully, it really does work wonders.

## B. Tips to Get Started with Time Blocking

Creating an effective time blocking schedule requires careful planning and preparation. Here are some tips for creating a successful time blocking schedule:

1. Before creating your time blocking schedule, determine your goals and priorities for the day or even the week if you are planning hat far ahead. This will help you prioritise tasks and ensure that your schedule is aligned with your desired outcomes. Why not use the method we talked about earlier and label your tasks High, Medium and Low to help you with this?

2. Assess your typical day and determine how much time you typically spend on various activities. This will help you understand how you currently use your time and where you can make changes to improve efficiency. Consider breaking up larger tasks to multiple blocks throughout the day. I split my household chores up as it helps avoid burnout by doing too much physical stuff all at once.

3. Plan your time blocking schedule, dedicating specific blocks of time to specific tasks or activities. Consider starting with blocks for work, exercise, self-care, and personal activities, and adjust as

needed. This part will take some juggling so try a different variety of layouts, put your self-care in the evening when the kids are in bed. Do your cleaning when they are at school. Just remember this is personal and what works for you may not be the same for someone else. Practice, and make the changes you need for it to be a success.

4. When creating your time blocking schedule, be realistic about how much time you can dedicate to each task. Overloading your schedule with too many tasks can lead to burnout and decreased efficiency. You only have a specific number of hours a day so get real and only set yourself up to smash the goals you know you can manage.

5. Time blocking schedules should be flexible, allowing for changes and adjustments as needed. Building in flexibility will help you manage unexpected events and changes in priorities, improving overall efficiency. This is called LIFE! If you have a sick day, that's okay. Be honest with yourself and clear your schedule if you need to rest. Doing a task for the sake of it does not mean you will do it well!

6. Regularly review and adjust your time blocking schedule as needed. As your goals and priorities change, your schedule should be adjusted to reflect these changes. At first you may need to juggle it throughout the day, but as you become more comfortable with the method, you will need to

refer to it less and less. I have been doing it for years now. And when my reminder alarm goes off at 11.00am on a Tuesday I have a brief glance at my planner to check, but I know it's my laundry block.

Creating an effective time blocking schedule requires careful planning and preparation. By determining your goals, assessing your typical day, planning your schedule, being realistic, building in flexibility, and regularly reviewing and adjusting as needed. I want you to know that you can create a successful time blocking schedule and it will work for you if you give it chance.

# VI. Putting it All Together

## A. Putting the Concepts into Practice

As we come the end of the book I wanted to provide you with a step-by-step guide for putting the concepts of "Slay Your Day," into practice:

*Determine your goals:* Before putting the concepts in the book into practice, determine your goals and priorities. This will help you understand what you want to achieve and ensure that your efforts are aligned with your wants and needs.

*Start waking up early*: Gradually adjust your sleep schedule to allow for early rising. Start by setting your alarm just 5 minutes earlier each day until you are waking up at your goal.

*Practice mindfulness*: Incorporate mindfulness practices into your morning routine, such as meditation or deep breathing, to help improve focus and reduce stress.

*Create a to-do list:* Create a to-do list each day, including tasks, appointments, and activities. Prioritise tasks based on importance with the High, Medium, Low technique, and adjust the list as needed throughout the day.

*Declutter your space:* Declutter your workspace and personal space to reduce distractions and improve organisation. Start with just one items a day if you need to and you will be surprised how addictive this becomes!

*Implement time blocking:* Dedicate specific blocks of time to specific tasks or activities. Start with blocks for work, exercise, self-care, and personal activities, and adjust as needed. This has been the biggest game changer for me in our lives, I cannot recommend enough how much you should give this a try.

*Minimise distractions:* Reduce distractions by minimising screen time and minimising interruptions. Set boundaries and communicate them to others to ensure that your focus remains intact.

*Regularly review and adjust:* Regularly review and adjust your schedule and to-do list as needed. This will help you stay on track and ensure that your efforts are aligned with your goals and priorities. Life happens, changes happen and you ned to be able to amend accordingly to allow for this.

By following these steps, I know you can effectively implement the concepts of the book, and have your best possible day, every day.

## B. Tips for Staying on Track

Just a few tips and tricks here to remind you to stay on track and keep at it:

*Stay accountable:* Hold yourself accountable for your actions and decisions. Create accountability systems, such as daily check-ins with a friend or accountability partner, to ensure that you are staying on track and making progress towards your goals. I take time daily to review the status of my life goals and make sure that my priorities and plans are aligned with my goals.

*Reward yourself:* Celebrate your successes and reward yourself for your hard work. You are smashing it, so give yourself a pat on the back! A little treat is a great way to make this whole experience more rewarding A bubble bath, face mask or glass of wine can be worth the wait at the end of a long but productive day. This will help you stay motivated and stay on track.

*Prioritise self-care*: Prioritise self-care and make time for rest, exercise, and relaxation. This will help you maintain energy levels and reduce stress. Add time blocks if you need to because this is an important part of the process.

*Surround yourself with support*: Surround yourself with supportive individuals who encourage and motivate you. Seek out mentorship and guidance from experienced individuals who can provide you with valuable insights and advice.

# VII. Conclusion

## A. Summary

This book provides advice on how to have your best day and best life possible through organisation, early rising, focus, and time blocking. These themes are critical for achieving success, reducing stress, and leading a fulfilling life.

Organisation provides a clear structure and helps you prioritise their tasks, leading to increased efficiency and reduced stress. Simple techniques, such as creating to-do lists and decluttering, can greatly improve your organisational skills.

Waking up early has numerous benefits, including increased energy levels and reduced stress. By following practical tips, such as setting a consistent sleep schedule and gradually adjusting your wake-up time, you can become an early rises and reap the benefits of waking up early.

Focus is essential for productivity and helps you avoid distractions and stay on task. Common distractions, such as screens and social media, can be overcome through techniques such as mindfulness and reducing screen time.

Time blocking is a valuable tool for managing time effectively and making the most of your day. By breaking down your day into focused blocks of time

34

and Prioritising tasks, individuals can improve their focus, increase productivity, and achieve your desired outcomes.

By incorporating these habits into your daily routine, you can lead a fulfilling and productive life, and have their best day possible. This is the definition of 'Slay Your Day!'

## B. What Are You Waiting For?

The time is now to take control of your day and start living your best life. "Slay Your Day" provides you with the tools and techniques you need to make positive changes in your life, reduce stress, and increase your productivity.

So, what are you waiting for? Make a commitment to yourself today and start implementing the concepts outlined in this book. Wake up early, prioritise your tasks, focus on what's important, and start slaying your day.

Remember, the power to create the life you want is within you. Take action today, be patient and consistent, and watch as the benefits of living a well-organised, focused, and productive life become evident.

Don't let another day go by without making positive changes in your life. It's time to "Slay Your Day" and start living your best life.

# Get Your Planner

## Available on Amazon!

# About The Author

Olivia Murray is a renowned authority on Law of Attraction, self-love, and confidence. She is a multi-talented individual as a YouTuber, author, public speaker, and podcast host. Olivia's impactful work has transformed the lives of hundreds of thousands of people, helping them turn their dreams into reality.

She empowers women to trust their instincts and seize opportunities by taking charge of their lives. She inspires them to publish their own books, launch their own podcasts, host their own events, and design their lives to match their aspirations.

Olivia guides women entrepreneurs in refining their unique voice and becoming influential leaders in their respective fields. Her message of empowerment resonates with women from all cultures and backgrounds, breaking down barriers and promoting equal opportunities globally.

# If You Enjoyed
# This Book

Please consider leaving a review on Amazon!

As a self-employed, self-publishing creative, reviews are essential to get my content out for more people to enjoy.

**Your review can make a huge difference!**

Thank you for being here until the end, and keep your eyes peeled for my …

**NEW BOOKS COMING SOON!**

Printed in Great Britain
by Amazon

23647683R00030